Everything You Ne(

YOUR PARENTS' DIVORCE

When a parent leaves home, life changes for everyone in the family.

• THE NEED TO KNOW LIBRARY •

Everything You Need to Know About YOUR PARENTS' DIVORCE

Linda Carlson Johnson

Series Editor: Evan Stark, Ph.D.

THE ROSEN PUBLISHING GROUP, INC.
NEW YORK

Published in 1989, 1992 by The Rosen Publishing Group, Inc.
29 East 21st Street, New York City, New York 10010

Revised Edition, 1992

Manufactured in the United States of America.

A Rosen Publishing Group classroom paperback distributed exclusively by Steck-Vaughn.

Library of Congress Cataloging-in-Publication Data

Johnson, Linda Carlson. 1949–
Everything you need to know about your parents' divorce / Linda Carlson Johnson. —Revised ed.
(The Need to know library)
Includes bibliographical references and index.
Summary: A guide for teenagers to view divorce as the beginning of a different kind of family life, to understand what happens to parents in their lives, and to understand the feelings of everyone involved.
ISBN 0-8114-3052-9
1. Divorce—Juvenile literature. [1. Divorce.] I. Title. II. Title: Your parents' divorce. III. Series.
HQ814.J57 1989
308.89—dc20 89-10268
CIP
AC

Contents

Introduction

No one who gets married plans to divorce. When people marry, they promise to stick with each other through good times and bad times. They intend to stay married to each other for life.

When that dream is shattered by divorce, there is always pain for the man and woman. Children feel the pain of divorce, too. Suddenly, a way of life, however good or bad it has been, is torn apart.

Have your parents divorced? If they have, you are probably still struggling in some ways with your pain. You may be angry with your parents. Or you may be confused about why the divorce happened. You may be holding on to the hope that somehow your parents will get back together. You may think that no one can possibly understand your pain.

This book will help you to face your feelings and understand how important it is to share them with other people. Your family life will never be the same again, but you still do have your mom and dad. With their help, you can build a new kind of family life with each of them. Many other people can help you to face your feelings so that the pain of divorce begins to heal.

Divorce may sometimes seem to you like a long nightmare that will never end. But with the help of people who care about you, you can wake up from that nightmare. Only then can you have dreams of your own.

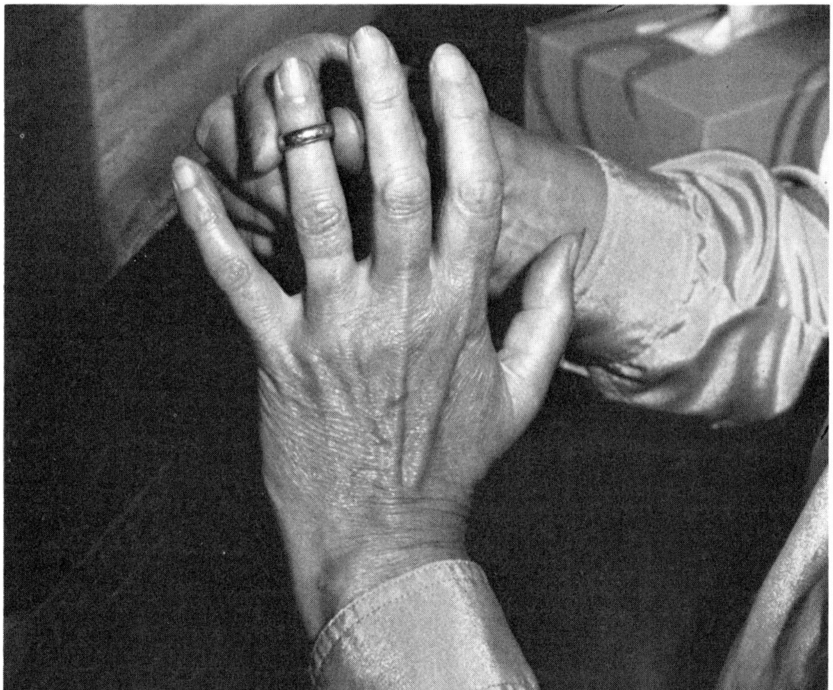

Children sometimes feel that a parent is leaving home because of them.

Chapter 1

Memories That Sting

Every day in the United States, about 3,000 kids become children of divorce. Kids don't often remember the day their parents signed the divorce papers. But they do remember the day they learned their parents were going to split up. Here is how four kids remember that painful day.

One day when I came home from school, I was surprised to see both of my parents' cars in the driveway. I opened the door. My father was slumped on the couch, his head in his hands. My mother was sitting on the floor. They looked up when they heard the door. I could see that they had both been crying.

My parents were screaming at each other again. But this time it was in the middle of the night, and it woke me up. I opened my bedroom door just as my mom walked past. Her face was bright red. She was yelling, "That's it! I'm out of here." She didn't even see me. She started down the stairs. My father came storming out of the bedroom after her. "You leave, and it's all over!" Mom kept going. She grabbed her coat and car keys and ran out the door. Then I heard the car engine.

Everybody always said that my mom and dad were the perfect couple. I thought so, too. They didn't fight like all my friends' parents. They always seemed so happy. But one day at dinner, they told me they were getting a divorce. I almost flipped out. I couldn't believe it. I still don't.

Things hadn't been right between my mom and dad for a long time. Mom seemed angry all the time. Dad seemed almost too nice, like he was guilty about something. He would try to hug my mom, but she wouldn't let him. Then one day, Dad came to my room. He told me that he and Mom were going to separate for a while. Later, Mom told me he'd gone to live with another woman.

One of these stories may sound just like what happened to you. Or your story might be different. But like most kids, you probably have memories of

It hurts to find out that parents don't love each other anymore.

your parents' breakup that still sting. It is the kind of day that is very hard to forget. You may still have bad feelings. It might help you to talk about those memories with someone you trust.

When one parent moves out children have to be more helpful a
home.

Chapter 2

Life Is Upside-Down

Everything in your life may seem upside-down because of your parents' divorce. Here are just a few of the things that you may be facing.

- **You probably live with either your mom or your dad most of the time now.**

In a divorce, one parent is usually given *custody*. That is, one parent is given the job of caring for a child and giving that child a place to live.

Often, the parents have joint custody of their children. *Joint custody* means that both parents take care of the children and make the decisions about them. Sometimes, especially when parents live near each other, kids live with one parent for part of the time and with another parent for part of the time.

In many cases, kids live with one parent, but the other parent has visitation rights. *Visitation rights* are rights given to a parent by a judge. These rights usually state how often a parent is allowed to see his or her children. Often, it's really kids who do the visiting; they live with one parent and go to stay with their other parent on weekends and school vacations, for example.

If you are unhappy with the arrangements the court or your parents have made, talk with your parents. They should know your feelings. You have a right to express yourself.

- **You may miss the parent you don't see as often.**

One of your parents may have moved far away. You may not be able to visit this parent very often. But you can keep in contact by phone. You and your parent can also write letters or exchange audio cassettes or videotapes.

What if your parent who lives far away doesn't make much effort to contact you? That can be very upsetting, especially if the two of you had been close. Contact with you may be painful for your parent. You bring back memories of a marriage that your parent is trying to forget. It may be best to try and contact your parent as often as you can yourself. Let your parent know that *you* still want to keep in touch.

- **You may be living in a new place.**

Some kids continue to live in the same house or apartment they lived in before their parents got divorced. But often, when parents split up, they have to sell their home or move into less expensive apartments.

Moving to a new place means more than just getting used to a new house. You'll probably have to get used to a new neighborhood. You may have to go to a different school, where you'll have to make new friends.

At first, these changes may seem too hard to handle. But time may change your feelings. You may come to like your new home just as much as you liked your old one.

- **Your mom and dad may have much less money.**

Your mom and dad have to pay for two places to live now instead of one. The parent who has custody of you may be getting some money, called *child support*, from your other parent. This money is used to help your parent pay for things like your food and clothing. Still, your mom and dad may have to struggle to pay their bills.

Stress about money can make people feel very upset. If you know your parents are having money trouble, you can help by not putting pressure on your parents to buy you expensive things. If you are old enough, you might consider getting a part-time job to try to help out with some of the bills.

- **Your parent may need help from you.**

You might have to take care of a younger brother or sister while your parent works. You might have to do more chores around the house too, such as taking care of the yard, fixing dinner, cleaning, or doing the laundry.

The most helpful thing you can do for your parent is to be cheerful. If you feel as if these extra jobs are getting to be too much, however, talk to your parent about it.

Talking to a neighbor or a friend about the divorce can be helpful.

Chapter 3

Why Blame Me?

Tom asks his mom for money for a new jean jacket. She says, "Forget it! I'm broke. Maybe if your father hadn't walked out on us, we would have the money."

Sara walks in the house, but her mother doesn't hear her. She is sitting at the kitchen table talking to her friend Joan. Joan says, "You didn't do anything wrong. You did everything for him. And what does he do to thank you? He just walks out. If you ask me, he was never good enough for you."

Bill is staying with his grandparents for a week. He hears them talking in the living room when they think he is asleep. "It's such a shame," his grandmother says. His grandfather says, "Yes, it's that wife of his. If she had not run around the way she did, they might still be together."

Tom, Sara, and Bill all have the same problem. People around them are angry. Often, when people are angry, they are feeling pain. And they want to find someone to blame for their pain.

If your parents are divorced, you may have heard many people blame one of them for what happened. Your mother or your father may be living in anger, blaming the other for the divorce. You may even feel strongly that one of your parents was more to blame for the divorce than the other.

It's very hard sometimes to deal with this kind of anger. Everyone wants to find someone to blame when something as tragic as divorce happens. Divorce can sometimes seem one-sided. But it is important to remember that divorce is almost never just one person's fault. It is also important to remember that this kind of anger hurts everyone. It hurts your mother and father and keeps them from rebuilding their lives. And it can "eat you up" inside.

If you can, you should try not to blame either your mother or your father for the divorce. That isn't always easy. But keep in mind that you don't know everything that led up to this divorce. Marriage is between two people. These people share joys, sorrows, and problems. You are part of their lives, but you don't know about all the private struggles your mother and your father may have had for a long time.

Children can be upset if grandparents take sides when parents argue.

What should you do if you still feel strongly that one of your parents is at fault in the divorce? Don't keep your feelings inside. Go to your mom or your dad and explain how you are feeling. Try to be calm. Tell your parent that you would really like to understand *why* this divorce happened. Try to keep an open mind, and be ready to forgive. Both of your parents probably made mistakes in their marriage. One parent may have hurt the other very badly. But staying angry at either one of them won't help. You need their love, and they need your love.

What if you can't stop feeling angry all the time about your parents' divorce? You may need help from someone besides your parents or relatives. The person you choose to talk to about your anger should be someone you trust. You might try talking to a school guidance counselor, a doctor, school psychologist, or someone at your church or synagogue. Be honest about your feelings. And be willing to at least listen to their suggestions.

Chapter 4

Is the Divorce My Fault?

Many kids don't blame their mother or father for a divorce. They blame themselves. Dwayne, Rae Ann, and Jennifer are three kids who think they caused their parents to break up.

- Dwayne is 16. He remembers what things were like before the divorce. His parents fought all the time. Most of the fights were about him. He was always in trouble.
- Rae Ann is 14. She always fought with her sister Stacey. Her dad would blow up just about every night. He would say, "I work all day and I come home to this? I should have stayed at work!"
- Jennifer is 13. Her mom said she and Jennifer's dad were happy once. She said everything changed when the kids came along.

Sometimes children think that a parent leaves home because they made the parent angry.

These kids blame themselves for different reasons. Dwayne saw his parents fighting about him all the time. He thought those fights caused the divorce. Rae Ann knew her fights with her sister made her father angry. She thought that if she hadn't been so bad, her father might have stayed. Jennifer didn't know what she had done. She just knew her mom seemed unhappy to have kids. Jennifer wished she had never been born.

What did these kids do about their feelings?

- Dwayne became very angry with himself. He took his anger out on everyone and everything around him. He got in fights all the time. He drank. He took drugs. He wouldn't do anything his mother said. He got drunk and wrecked his father's car.
- Rae Ann and her sister visited her father every weekend. Rae Ann never said anything. She was afraid she would start fighting with Stacey. Rae Ann's dad couldn't understand what was wrong.
- Jennifer got very depressed. She felt sick all the time. She stopped talking to her friends. One day, she tried to kill herself. She took as many pills as she could find. Her mom found her lying on the bedroom floor. She rushed Jennifer to the hospital. Jennifer had to have her stomach pumped out. When Jennifer woke up, she cried. She said she wished she had died.

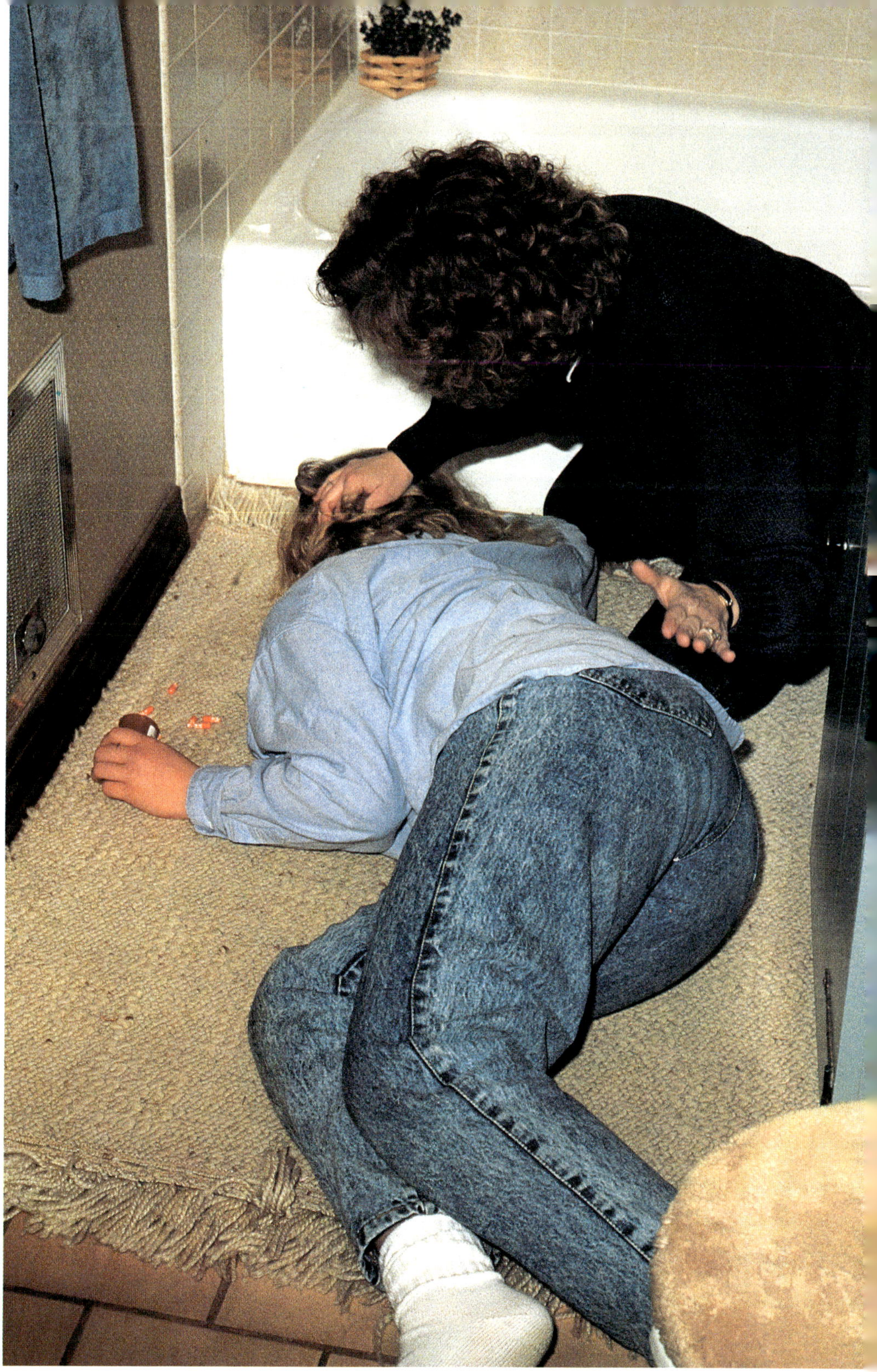

When parents divorce, some children get very depressed and try to commit suicide.

None of these kids caused their parents to split up. But they thought they did. They became angry, afraid, and sad. They couldn't go on with their lives until they got help. All three did get help.

- Dwayne had to go to a special school for troubled kids. The counselors there helped him with his drinking and drug problems. They found out how Dwayne felt about his parents' divorce. Then the counselors talked to Dwayne and his parents. Dwayne learned the divorce was not his fault. Dwayne's parents learned about ways to help Dwayne.

- Rae Ann finally talked to her dad about what was bothering her. He told her that the divorce wasn't her fault at all. Then Rae Ann wasn't afraid to talk to Stacey when their dad was around.

- Jennifer's mom told her more about the divorce. Jennifer found out there were many reasons for the divorce. Jennifer's mom and dad both told her how much they loved her. They made sure she knew the divorce was not her fault. They began spending more time with Jennifer and her brothers.

Do you blame yourself for your parents' divorce? You may think you did something to make the divorce happen. Or you may just feel angry or sad all the time.

It is important to remember that your parents' divorce is not your fault. Your parents may have said things they didn't really mean. They may have fought about you. They may have been angry with you. But divorce is not between parents and children. It is between a husband and wife.

If you blame yourself for your parents' divorce, don't keep your feelings inside. If you can talk to your mom or dad, do that.

Tell your mom or dad how you are feeling. You might say, "Dad (or Mom), there's something that has been bothering me." You might say, "Mom (or Dad), I've been feeling very upset ever since the divorce. But I'm not upset with you. I'm upset with me."

Then you should tell your mom or dad that you blame yourself for the divorce. Try to tell your mom or dad exactly why you feel this way.

Most of the time, talking to your parents is the best thing to do. But that may be too hard for you to do. If it is, talk to another adult you trust. Do not keep your feelings to yourself.

Sometimes divorced parents try to buy a child's love with presents.

Chapter 5

A Tug of War

After a divorce, parents must start new lives apart. But they still share children. So the parents must see and talk with each other.

Sometimes, parents are still friends after their divorce. They talk to each other about their kids. They set rules for their kids to follow in mom's house and dad's house. They agree not to say bad things about each other to their kids.

But sometimes, divorced parents are not friendly to each other. They are still angry. They may not talk to each other very much. But they do talk to their kids. These parents say bad things about each other. They try to get the kids to agree with those things. Kids may feel they are in the middle of a tug-of-war between their mother and father.

Sometimes parents try to get their kids to take sides for another reason. They are afraid of losing their kids' love. Then parents may try to do things to "buy" love. They may take their kids to special places. They may buy them very expensive things. Or they may let their kids do whatever they want to do.

When one parent does these things, the other parent may be very upset. Again, the kids are in the middle of a tug-of-war.

What should you do if your parent tries to get you to take sides?

- If your parents say bad things about each other, tell them you don't want to hear those things. You might say, "I know how you feel. But please don't talk that way any more. I still love my dad (or mom)."
- If one parent tries to "buy" your love, be careful. You might feel good about getting presents or going to special places. But don't be fooled. These things are not what love is about. You should also let your other parent know that you love him or her.

The most important thing to remember is: Don't take sides. You need both of your parents' love to help you through this hard time. And to help you grow up happy and strong. Let them know that.

Special Cases

Sometimes, parents may do things that are harmful to themselves or someone else. Then you may have to stay away from them until they get help. Or you may have to tell someone what they are doing so they can get help. Here are some of the things a parent might do.

• **Get drunk or high on drugs all the time.** If your parent has a drinking or drug problem, you won't be able to help. Talk to an adult you trust about the problem.

• **Become violent.** If your parent tries to hurt you or your other parent, you should call the police. They are trained to help.

• **Act very depressed.** After a divorce, parents can be very upset. That's normal. But sometimes a mom or dad may seem to want to die. If one of your parents talks about suicide, tell another adult.

An unhappy parent might become violent.

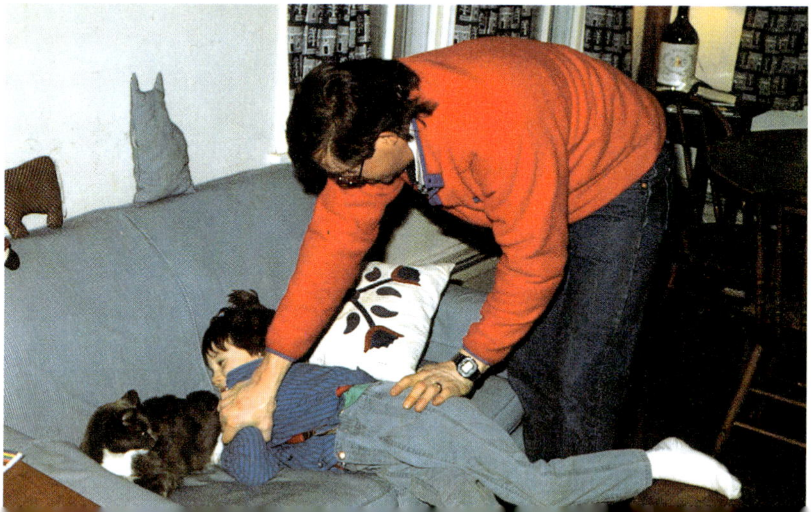

Helping a parent through difficult times can be an extra burden for young people.

Chapter 6

Grow Up, Mom and Dad!

Tom calls Sue for a date on Saturday night. Sue turns him down. She says she has to stay home because her mother needs her.

Eric visits his dad on weekends. His dad always takes him out to bars with him. Eric's dad usually gets drunk. Eric has to drive him home. Then Eric helps his dad undress and puts him to bed.

Sharnelle can't go anywhere anymore. When she comes home, the house is a mess. Her mother is always curled up in her bedroom with a book. Sharnelle has to do all the cleaning and cooking.

The parents of these kids are acting like children. They don't want to face their lives alone. Sue's mom is afraid to be alone. Eric's dad expects Eric to take care of him. Sharnelle's mom doesn't want to act like an adult anymore. She wants to stay in her room.

When parents act like children, children often have to act like parents. But sometimes this goes too far. Then the children don't have lives of their own anymore.

What should you do if this happens to you? First, you should try to talk to the parent who is causing the problem for you. When you do, try not to sound too angry. Your parent may listen better if you are calm. Here is how this talk might go for Sue, Eric and Sharnelle.

- Sue might say, "Mom, I really miss my friends. I would like to go out this Saturday night. I know you don't like to be alone. Is there someone else you could ask to come over?"

- Eric might say, "Dad, I love you but I'm worried about you. You seem to be drinking more and more. That makes me scared. I wish you would stop. Maybe we could go to a movie instead of to a bar next weekend."

It is important for children to communicate with their divorced parents.

- Sharnelle might say, "Mom, I'm tired. I understand that you are sad. But I can't handle my schoolwork and all the housework too. Could you help me with dinner tonight?"

If this talk doesn't help, you might need to go to someone else. Try talking to another adult in the family who you think might understand. Call your clergyman or school guidance counselor. These people might be able to help. They may help you find ways to talk to your parents. They may even talk to your parents for you. If you *don't* want them to do that, you should say so.

Being separated from the family can create feelings of guilt.

Chapter 7

A Weekend Parent

You're living with your mom. Your father picks you up and takes you out to dinner. It's a disaster. You don't know what to say to him, and he doesn't know what to say to you. You wish you could be anywhere else but here.

After a divorce, nothing is normal. When you lived with both your parents, they saw you every day. There was a routine, a set way of doing things. Your mother and father each did many of the same things every day, and so did you. You probably talked casually while you did the dishes or while you watched TV. You may never have spent an evening out with just one of your parents.

Seeing one of your parents only once in a while can be difficult. Your parent may suddenly seem like a stanger to you. Even if you want to talk to your parent, it can be hard to find something to say. Things don't feel right.

Your mom or dad may also be trying *too* hard to entertain you. On each visit, your parent may be stretching to find special things the two of you can do together. Each weekend, it may be a new adventure—a movie, dinner, a trip to the city, shopping at the mall. Or you may stay at your parent's home, watching video after video. You may even find that your parent is suddenly buying you everything you ask for.

What has changed? Your parent may be feeling guilty because the family has broken up. He or she may be trying to repair the damage. Or your parent may simply want to show you his or her love.

If you feel uncomfortable about the way things are between you and your mom or dad, try talking things out. Tell your parent that every visit doesn't have to be a special occasion. Tell your parent that there's no need to entertain you; suggest that the two of you just hang out together.

Building a new relationship with a parent who no longer lives at home takes work. But if you love one another, you'll both want to give it a try. Things between you may become even better than before the divorce.

Chapter 8

Why Can't They Get Back Together?

It had been a year since Heather's parents divorced. Her mom and dad seemed to get along so well. They talked on the phone all the time. When Dad came to pick Heather up, Mom always met him at the door. They seemed happy to see each other, and they always talked for a while. Once, Mom even asked Dad in for coffee.

After the divorce, Sam went to live with his father. He really missed his mom. He talked all the time about things they had done together as a family. Dad listened, but he didn't say anything.

Jason hasn't talked to his father since the divorce. It has been six months. Jason made a promise to himself. He would not talk to his dad until his dad came back home for good.

Heather, Sam, and Jason love their parents. They are like many kids who want their parents to get back together. They don't understand why their parents got a divorce. Even if they do know why, they choose not to remember. Instead, they think of the good times they had as a family. They think all their problems would be over if only their mom and dad would get back together.

Often, kids can't accept their parents' divorce.

- Some kids tell their parents how they feel. A kid might yell, "Why can't you two work this out? It's not fair! I want everything back to normal!"
- Some kids keep their feelings inside. But they secretly hope that their parents will get back together. They watch for any little sign of love between their parents.
- Some kids act as if they don't want their parents to get back together even when they really do. A kid who feels this way might say, "I don't care about this divorce. It's your problem, not mine." But inside, this kid may be feeling hurt and angry. He or she is wishing the divorce had never happened.
- Some kids don't really become angry about their parents' divorce until some years later. When a divorced mom moves away or remarries, for example, her child may suddenly ask, "How can you leave? What about Dad? Don't you love him?"

A family can still get along together, even if the parents are divorced.

Have you had a hard time accepting your parents' divorce? You're not alone. Many kids feel this way. But it is important for you to understand that your mom and dad will probably not get back together.

It is not unusual to feel alone and confused after a divorce.

Chapter 9

Nobody Understands

Juan used to have a lot of friends. He was on the basketball team. He got good grades. He always had a smile for everyone. Then Juan's parents got a divorce. Juan was out of school often. He walked with his head down. He quit the basketball team. He started to get into fights. At first, his friends called him every night. Juan wouldn't even come to the phone. After a while, they stopped calling.

Juan feels as if no one else understands his problems. He thinks no one has ever felt as bad as he feels now. He doesn't think he will ever be happy again. He feels very much alone.

You may feel alone too. But you are not. About three out of every ten kids have been through a divorce. That means that in a class of 30 kids, 9 of them probably have divorced parents. Some live with just their mom or dad. Some live with a stepparent too.

Talking to someone who has been through a divorce may help you feel better. If none of your friends have divorced parents, talk to your school counselor. He or she may know of a *support group* that can help you. A support group is a group of people who get together to talk about their problems. They help, or support, each other.

Other friends may help too. If you have a best friend, you should talk to him or her. Sometimes it helps just to have someone who will listen.

It is also important to keep busy. Try not to think about your problems all the time. Instead, go to that basketball practice. Do your homework. Go out with your friends. Doing these things won't solve your problems. But at least you can keep them out of your mind for a while.

If you still feel down, tell your mom or dad or someone else you trust. Remember, you do not have to be alone.

Chapter 10

When Parents Date

John's mother walked into the living room in a new dress. She was all made up and was wearing perfume.

"How do I look?" she asked John.

"Where are you going?" John asked.

"Out with a man I met at work. So how do I look?" his mom asked again.

"Does Dad know about this?" John asked.

"No, of course not. John, your dad and I have been divorced for six months." His mom sounded frustrated.

"Yeah, I know, but . . ." John started to say.

"But I shouldn't date?" his mom interrupted.

"Oh, do whatever you want." John was almost yelling. He stomped up the stairs.

"John," his mother called after him. John's answer was to slam his door.

John is 15. He is very upset with his mother. He doesn't really even understand why. But he feels that his mother is cheating on his father.

John's mother isn't doing that. She is a single woman, and she felt attracted to a man. She decided to go out with him. But John has a hard time understanding why his mother wants to do that. He hasn't really accepted that his parents are divorced.

Shana's dad said he had to talk with her about something. He said he was going out with a woman on Friday night.

"How old is she?" Shana asked.

"Is that important?" her dad asked.

"Yes," Shana said.

"She's 28," her dad said.

"Twenty-eight? She's ten years younger than Mom! What does she look like?" Shana said.

"She's nice looking," her dad said.

"Is she prettier than Mom?" Shana asked.

"I wouldn't compare them," Shana's dad answered.

"Are you going to sleep with her?" Shana asked.

"Shana!" Her dad sounded shocked. "Why would you say a thing like that?"

Shana started to cry.

Shana is 14. Her dad's date has upset her. She feels that her dad is not just her dad any more. He

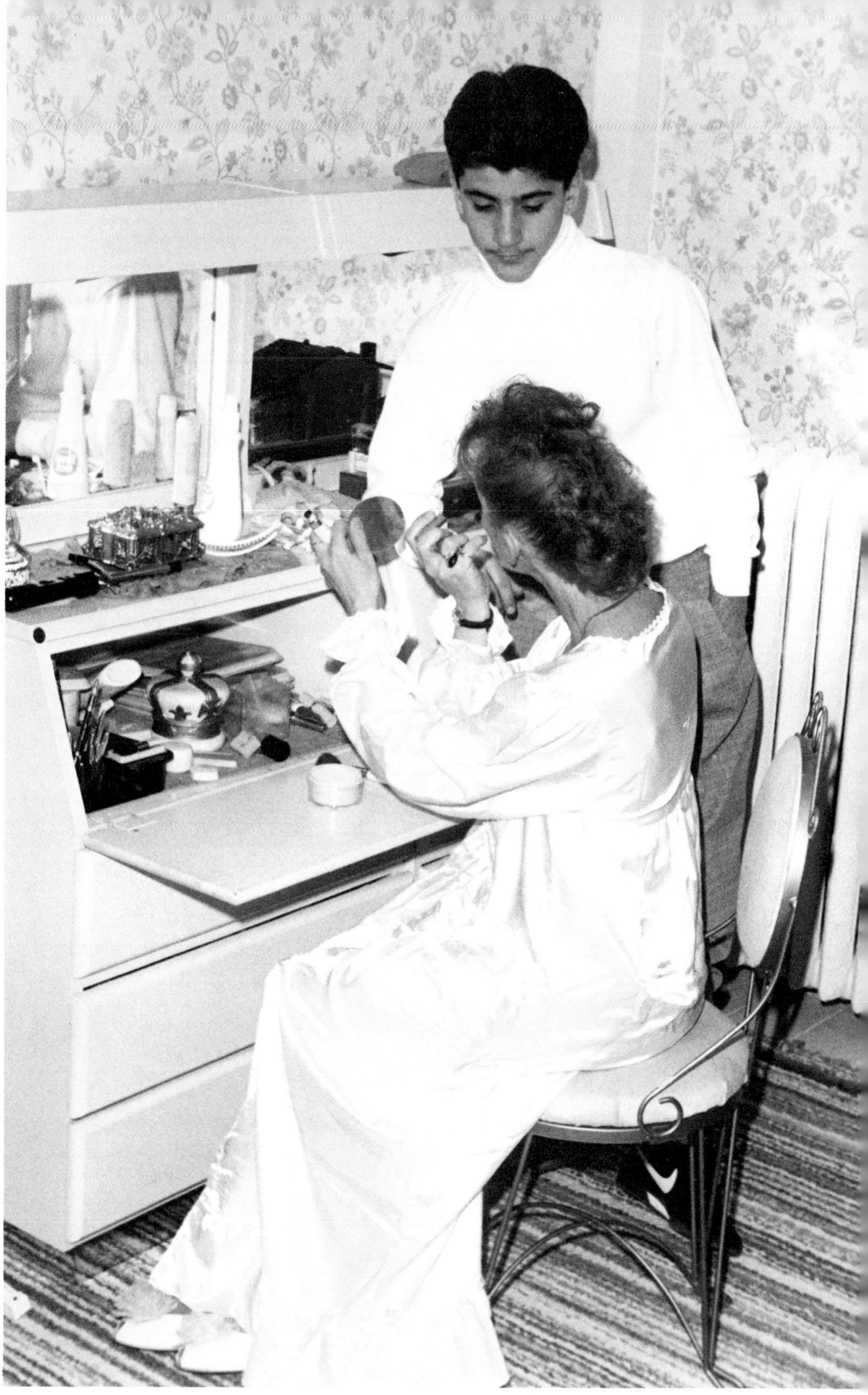

A child may object to a parent dating and meeting new partners.

is a man who goes out with women. Shana herself is becoming a woman. She knows what it is like to feel attracted to a boy. It is hard for her to think about her dad having feelings like that for a woman. It is especially hard for her to think about her dad being with a woman other than her mom. Shana also feels very close to her dad. She feels that this young, attractive woman may take her dad away from her.

Shana is very confused. In one way, she understands her father's need to date. But in another way, she is angry about it. And she is afraid too.

If your divorced parents are dating, you may feel some of the things John and Shana felt. It's not easy to see your mom and dad as single people. But that's what they are. They are trying to start new lives. That means they will make new friends. And they will probably date.

When that happens, you may be confused or upset. If you are, there are a few things you should *not* do.

- You should not yell at your mom or dad. If you do, your mom or dad may scream right back at you. Then no one will feel any better.

- You should not tell your mom or dad what to do either. If you do, they may tell you to stay out of their personal lives. You will still feel bad, but you won't be able to talk to your parents about your feelings.

- You should not talk about your feelings in front of your mom's or dad's date. You may make the date feel very upset. And you may make your mom or dad angry.

What *should* you do about your feelings? Talk to your mom or dad. When you do, try to stay calm. It's okay to say that you are upset. But try not to *act* upset. You might say, "I know you are single now. But it really bothers me to see you with someone besides Mom (or Dad). I don't know why I feel this way, but I do."

Even if you are calm, your mom or dad may become angry. If that happens, say, "Maybe we shouldn't talk about this right now."

Talking this way to your mom or dad may be hard. It's especially hard if you and your parents often yell at each other. But it is best to stay calm. If *you* do, there is a better chance that your parents will stay calm too.

It may be difficult for a son or daughter to accept a new family member.

Chapter 11

When Parents Remarry

One day, your mom or dad may decide to marry again. That day could come very soon. Or it may never come at all. If that day does come, it will be an important day for you too. It will mean big changes in your life. Here are five stories about kids whose parents decided to marry again.

Seth is very troubled. He hasn't had much time to understand his parents' divorce. Now he has to get used to a stepfather too.

Seth's mom was divorced one week and married the next. Seth knew that would happen. His mom had left his dad because of Jerry. But it all seemed to happen so fast. His mom and Jerry went away together for a week, then they came home.

Jerry told Seth he wouldn't try to replace Seth's father. But in just a few days, Jerry was telling Seth what to do. Seth wanted to leave home, but he couldn't. He was only 14. He called his dad and asked if he could stay with him. But Seth's dad said he couldn't afford an apartment big enough for the two of them.

Janice didn't mind it that her mom dated. At least, not until Chuck came along.

Janice's mom had been dating for a year. But in all that time, she had not brought her dates home. She always met her date at a restaurant. Then one night Janice's mom invited a man named Chuck to dinner. She and Chuck told Janice that they were going to be married.

Later that night, Janice's mom asked Janice if she liked Chuck. Janice didn't like him at all. He wasn't at all like her dad. He laughed too loud, and he swore all the time. But Janice didn't tell her mother how she felt. Her mother seemed so happy.

Justine was happy when her dad married Esther. But then Esther and her two boys moved in.

Justine liked Esther all right. That wasn't the problem. It was Esther's two stupid sons that drove Justine crazy. They were 9 and 11 years old and nothing but trouble.

Justine's dad said she should give the boys a chance. She tried. But the boys didn't try back. They called her a pig, and they said rotten things about her boyfriend. Justine hated them so much that she began to hate Esther too. Then she even began to hate her dad for marrying Esther.

Joe and his dad had never been very close. So Joe was happy when Stu came into his mother's life.

Joe liked Stu from the first time they met. That was about a year after the divorce. Stu took Joe and Joe's mom to a hockey game. They had a great time together. When Stu came over to the house, he always had time for Joe. They played catch in the yard. Sometimes they just sat on the porch and talked. So Joe was very happy when his mom and Stu got married.

Sherry didn't know that when her dad remarried, she would feel so left out.

Sherry lived with her mom during the week and her dad on weekends. Sherry and her dad always had a great time. But then Sherry's dad married Kathryn. Sherry didn't feel wanted at her dad's house anymore. Every weekend that she visited was worse.

At first, Kathryn just gave Sherry dirty looks when Sherry's dad wasn't watching. Then Kathryn started to boss Sherry around. She told Sherry that she should learn some manners. Every time Sherry touched anything in the house, Kathryn yelled at her.

Sherry tried to talk to her dad about Kathryn. But her dad wouldn't listen. He kept taking Kathryn's side. Sherry started finding reasons to stay with her mom on weekends.

For Sherry, her dad's marriage is terrible. Sherry feels as if she has lost her dad—again. She is glad she gets along really well with her mom. For Joe, his mom's marriage is great. He feels as if he has found a dad—at last. Quite often, things turn out this way. Seth, Janice, and Justine aren't very happy with what has happened in their parents' lives. But in time, things may get better for them.

Each of these kids' stories is special. If your mom or dad decides to remarry, another special story will begin. That story will be yours.

For Sherry, her dad's marriage is terrible. Sherry feels as if she has lost her dad—again.

Chapter 12

Hope for the Future

Like many kids, you may be having a hard time getting over your parents' divorce. But as many kids have found out, the pain of divorce lessens with time. As you struggle to find a new kind of life with your mom and dad, try to remember:

- You may be angry with your parents right now, but remember that you have only *one* father and *one* mother. You need their love, and they need yours, too.

- Try not to keep thinking about who was to blame for the divorce. Many people may be ready to blame either your mother or your father

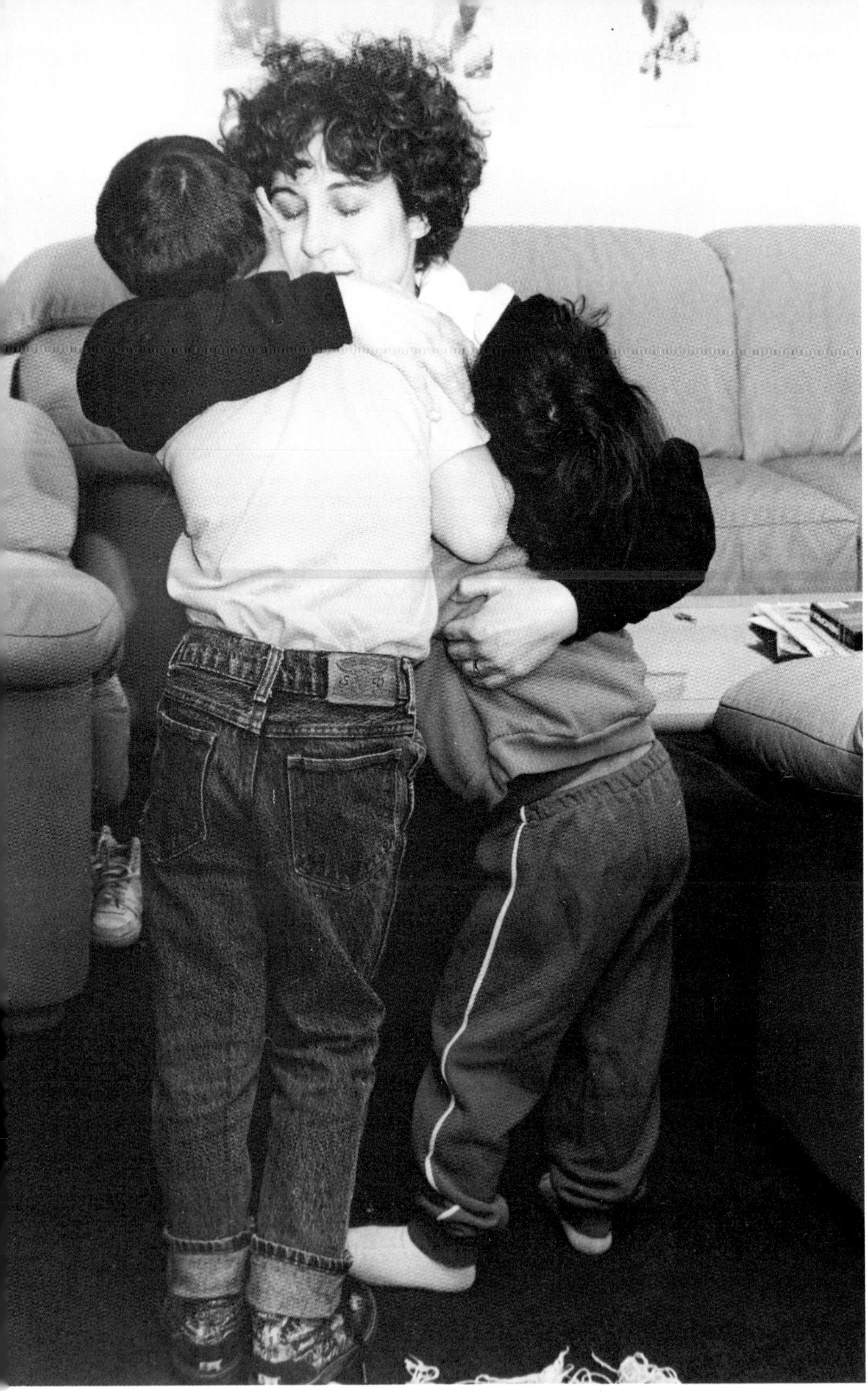

A divorce does not change the love between parents and children.

The most important thing to remember is this: You are not alone.

for what happened. One of your parents may blame the other for the divorce. But you don't know all the reasons for what happened. It's best for you to avoid taking sides.

- *You* are not to blame for your parents' divorce. Divorce, like marriage, is between two people.

- Your parents will probably not get back together. You need to let go of the past.

- Talk to your parents about your feelings. Let them know when you are upset or sad.

- Try to understand that, like you, your parents are trying to build new lives. They may begin dating other people. They may even remarry someday.

Above all, remember that you are not alone. Many kids have gone through the pain of their parents' divorce. And many people who understand what you are going through are ready to help you. All you have to do is reach out to them. They can help you to find ways to deal with your pain. Then you can put this divorce behind you and begin to look toward the future with hope.

Glossary—*Explaining New Words*

blame To find fault with someone or something.

child support Money the supporting parent must pay to the other after a divorce. The money is used to help pay for the children's food, clothes, and other expenses.

clergyman A minister, priest, or rabbi.

custody Care and control over children after a divorce. Joint custody means that both parents must care for the children and make decisions about them.

depressed Very sad. If you are just a little depressed, you might say that you feel "down." If you are very depressed, you may need to see a doctor for help.

suicide The act of taking your life (killing yourself) on purpose.

support group People who have problems that are alike and who get together to help each other.

violent Excited, usually in anger, so that you lose control. A storm that causes a lot of damage is called a violent storm. A person who is violent may try to harm someone nearby.

visitation rights Rules about how often and when parents who do not live with children may see them. These rights are usually written down by a judge at the time of a divorce.

Where to Get Help

If you feel down, you should talk to an adult you trust. That person might be a teacher, a counselor, a clergyman or someone in your family. But there are times when you may need special help. You may feel that you want to die. Or you may feel that you want to run away from home.

If you feel this way, look in the Yellow Pages of your phone book. Look for the words CRISIS CENTER or MENTAL HEALTH CENTER. Or call your local hospital's emergency room. Someone there may be able to help.

If you feel as if you want to die, or you think one of your parents may commit suicide, there is another way to find help. Call 1-800-555-1212. Ask the operator for the number of a SUICIDE HOTLINE. The operator will give you another number to call that begins with 1-800. (There is no charge for calling "800" numbers.)

If one of your parents harms you or tries to harm you, call the National Child Abuse Hotline, 1-800-333-7233.

For Further Reading

Fayerweather Street School, The Unit. Rofer, Eric E., ed. *The Kids' Book of Divorce.* Lexington, Mass.: The Lewis Publishing Co., 1981, 123 pages. This book was put together by 20 students, ages 11 to 14. They talk about how and why divorce happens and give ideas about how to feel better after a divorce.

Krementz, Jill. *How It Feels When Parents Divorce.* New York: Alfred A. Knopf, 1984, 115 pages. In this book, young people from age 7 to 16 share their feelings about their parents' divorces.

Mann, Peggy. *My Dad Lives in a Downtown Hotel.* Garden City, New York: Doubleday & Company, Inc., 96 pages. *(Fiction)* This is a story about a boy named Joey. He becomes closer to his father after his parents get a divorce.

Okimoto, Jean Davies. *My Mother Is Not Married to My Father.* New York: G.P. Putnam's Sons, 1981, 109 pages. (*Fiction*) This story is told by a girl named Cynthia. Her parents are divorced, and she doesn't like her dad's girlfriend.

Sobol, Harriet Langsam. *My Other-Mother, My Other-Father.* New York: Macmillan Publishing Co., Inc., 1979, 34 pages. This book is about a girl whose divorced parents marry other people.

Stenson, Janet Sinberg. *Now I have a Stepparent and it's kind of confusing*. New York: Avon Books, 1979, 36 pages. This book is about a boy whose mother marries again after a divorce.

Index

About the Author

Linda Carlson Johnson taught junior high and high school English for nine years before embarking on a second career in publishing. She has reported for a daily newspaper in New Hampshire and a weekly newspaper in Old Lyme, Connecticut. She is now a senior editor of the national children's newspaper, *Weekly Reader.* Ms. Johnson's other books include *Mother Teresa, Barbara Jordan, Patriotism, Responsibility, Our Constitution,* and *Our National Symbols.*

About the Editor

Evan Stark is a well-known sociologist, educator, and therapist as well as a popular lecturer on women's and children's health issues. Dr. Stark was the Henry Rutgers Fellow at Rutgers University, an associate at the Institution for Social and Policy Studies at Yale University, and a Fulbright Fellow at the University of Essex. He is the author of many publications in the field of family relations and is the father of four children.

Acknowledgments and Photo Credits

Photographs by Stuart Rabinowitz

Design/Production: Blackbirch Graphics, Inc.
Cover Photograph: Stuart Rabinowitz